# SPRING VALLEY
# everywear

written by **Ellen Warwick** ✳ illustrated by **Bernice Lum**

Kids Can Press

For Madison — EW

For nimali, my SUPERbud ... much xxx — BL

Kids Can Press acknowledges the financial support of the Government of Ontario, through the Ontario Media Development Corporation's Ontario Book Initiative, and the Government of Canada, through the BPIDP, for our publishing activity.

Published in Canada by
Kids Can Press Ltd.
29 Birch Avenue
Toronto, ON  M4V 1E2

www.kidscanpress.com

Published in the U.S. by
Kids Can Press Ltd.
2250 Military Road
Tonawanda, NY  14150

Edited by Yvette Ghione
Designed by Karen Powers
Printed and bound in China

The paper used to print this book was produced with elemental chlorine-free pulp, harvested from managed sustainable forests.

CM 08  0 9 8 7 6 5 4 3 2 1

Library and Archives Canada Cataloguing in Publication

Warwick, Ellen
    Everywear / written by Ellen Warwick ; illustrated by Bernice Lum.

(Planet girl)
ISBN 978-1-55337-799-3

1. Handicraft for girls—Juvenile literature.
2. Dress accessories—Juvenile literature.
I. Lum, Bernice  II. Title.  III. Series.

TT560.W373 2008    j646.4'8    C2007-907015-9

Kids Can Press is a Corus™ Entertainment company

# Contents

# NEVER GO UNADORNED AGAIN!

*Wardrobe washed out? No punch to your* **PANACHE***? Done with the plain-Jane reputation? Accessories can take any look from* **SO-SO** *to* **SUPER***, adding that little something special to an ordinary ol' shopping mall outfit while making a personal style statement. You need to* **ACCESSORIZE YOUR LIFE***!*

*Anyone can buy the same accessories that everyone else does, but where's the* **FUN** *in that? Doll up your duds with your own* **UNIQUE CHIC***! Start with dazzling hair doodads to* **JAZZ UP** *your 'do and jewelry that'll make you* **SPARKLE** *without breaking the bank. Then give*

*your garb some get-up-and-go with* GREAT GEAR, *including knockout bags that'll send your* STYLE POWER *off the charts.*

*And these accessories are super* AFFORDABLE — *some may even be nearly* FREE *if you have the basics around the house, like newspaper, duct tape, chopsticks and glue.*

*Read on for all the stuff you need to know, stuff you gotta have and* PROJECTS *that* POP. *Get outta the wardrobe doldrums and* ACCESSORIZE YOURSELF!

# WHOA, GIRL!

Bet you're champing at the bit to get going, but rein your crafty self in for a quick sec. Check out this section for some super important things that'll not only save you some time and money, but will also save you some frustration, too.

It's a really good idea to read through each project's instructions before you start. It would be a huge drag to get stuck on something tricky partway through a project or — yikes! — find out you're missing something important.

Don't miss this section! There's a ton of important information here!

6

# Stuff to Use and How to Use It

Once you've read through the instructions, the next step is to gather up the stuff you need — the tools and materials. Before you step out the door, poke around your basement, your bedroom, the junk drawer and in all the nooks and crannies around the house where cool craft stuff might be tucked away. And if you don't find the exact thing on the list, you could use something else you've found to make it a one-of-a-kind original.

If you can't find everything in your search, most of the stuff you need is sold at craft or sewing supply stores. You'll probably need to head to a hardware or office supply store for a few things, too. Didn't think you'd ever buy craft materials there, did ya?! You'd be amazed at all the bits and bobs you can find! Wander the aisles and prepare to be inspired.

# Snaps versus Cap Snaps: Battle of the Fasteners

What's the diff between snaps and cap snaps? Well, they both fasten things together in the same way, but they look different on the outside of the project, and they're attached in totally different ways.

**Snaps** are sewn on so that you don't see them on the outside of the project. Simply separate the two halves and sew one onto each of the project's inside edges.

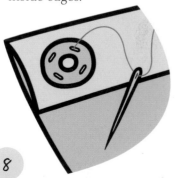

**Cap snaps** are a little more complicated to attach, but it's worth the extra effort. The cap part shows on the outside of the project and looks really cool. When you buy the cap snaps, you'll have to get a small snap-attaching tool, too. This small metal tool is used with a hammer. Ask an adult to help you follow these steps:

1. On the wrong side of the fabric, measure and make a mark where you want the snap to be.

2. On a protected surface, place the prong side of a snap half with the points facing up.

3. Press the fabric onto the prongs until the points poke through the fabric.

4. Put a socket over the prongs. Place the tool onto the snap and gently hammer the top of the tool until the prongs and socket are pressed tightly together.

Repeat steps 1 to 4 for the other snap half.

# GLUE GUN: HOW LOW CAN YOU GO?

Glue guns are either high temperature or low temperature. The low-temp ones work okay, but they don't always stick things together as well as the high-temp ones. The high-temp ones are hot, hot, HOT! They stick things together really well, but you've gotta be super careful if you use one. Definitely wear work gloves. Whichever kind of glue gun you go for, read the package directions and keep an adult nearby.

# UTILITY KNIFE: WATCH THOSE FINGERS!

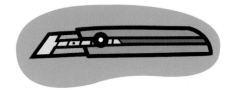

Be very careful when you're using one of these sharp tools. Ask permission first and keep that adult around while you're cutting stuff. And make sure to protect your work surface with a cutting mat, a magazine or a piece of corrugated cardboard — the knife will cut all the way through your material.

When cutting straight lines, hold a ruler down with one hand and keep the knife's blade against the ruler's edge. HEADS-UP: Keep your body parts out of the way — especially the fingers holding the ruler down.

# Pinking Shears

Nope, nothing to do with anything pink. These shears cut a nifty zigzag edge instead of the straight edge you get with regular scissors. You can find these at craft or sewing supply stores. If zigzag isn't your bag, you can get scissors that make other types of fancy cuts.

# Beading Stuff

There's nothing too complicated about the beading projects in this book, but here's a key to the lingo:

**Needlenose pliers:** These handy little pliers have pointy ends that can be used to pick up beads, bend wire or open and close loops. You can find them at any craft supply or hardware store.

**Ring forms:** These rings have a flat round or oval piece on top that you can glue things on.

**Clasps:** Lots of different types of clasps are available, such as spring rings, lobster clasps or barrel clasps. You can use whatever kind you like.

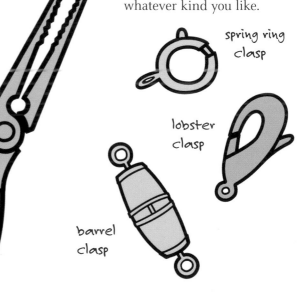

spring ring clasp

lobster clasp

barrel clasp

**Earring wires:** There are lots of different types of earring wires, too. Any kind will do. If you don't have pierced ears, you can find clip-on earring forms at most beading or craft supply stores.

**Head pins and eye pins:** Slip some beads onto either of these pins and leave enough space at the top to bend a small loop.

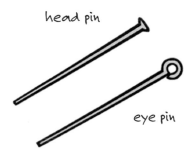

head pin

eye pin

**Crimps:** These teeny weeny tubes are great for attaching two pieces of beading wire together or making loops. Tuck two wire ends into a crimp and pinch it closed with needlenose pliers.

**Jump rings:** These little rings are used to link things together. Use needlenose pliers to gently pry the ends apart and then bring them back together to form a loop.

**Beading wire:** This soft, flexible wire comes on a spool and its thickness is measured by gauge. Any gauge will do for the "Pretty paper necklace" on page 36.

**Metal end caps:** Head to the beading store for these handy caps. They slip onto the ends of a project like the "Swish hair sticks" on page 20, and they have a ring on the top to attach other stuff to.

# Sew What? Stuff You Should Know

A bunch of the projects in the pages ahead use sewing. Sewing is a snap if you keep a few points in mind. You can sew all the projects by hand with a needle and thread, but if you want to use a sewing machine, that's cool, too — just ask for permission and a helping hand from an adult.

⊙ To start, here's a small but important tip about prepping your stuff for sewing: When you're pinning fabric together, the pins should be at right angles to the fabric edges. This is key when using a sewing machine; otherwise, the pins will get caught up in the machine and mess everything up. Also, it helps to remove the pins as you sew.

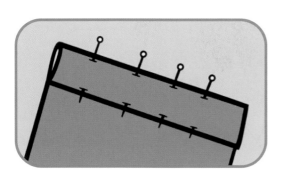

⊙ Whichever way you're sewing, make a few extra stitches at corners and when starting and ending your seams and hems. And to finish your sewing, tie a few knots close to the fabric and trim the extra thread. That way your project won't unravel after it's done!

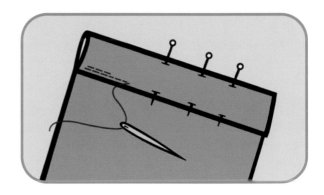

⊙ To sew by hand, cut a piece of thread about as long as your arm. Poke one end of the thread through the eye of a needle and pull it through about 10 cm (4 in.). Then, tie a knot at the other end of the thread.

## Running stitch

1. Starting about 1 cm (½ in.) from the edges of the fabric, poke the threaded needle up through the fabric until the knot catches. Then, poke it back down through the fabric a little way over.

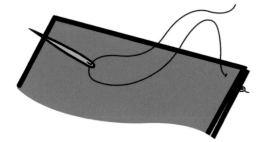

2. Continue poking the needle back up and then down through the fabric again in this way, keeping your stitches as even as you can. Watch that you don't pull the thread too tight as you go, or your fabric will bunch up.

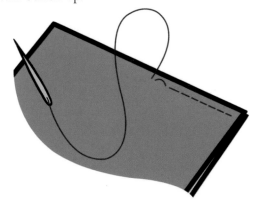

## Whipstitch

Sewing with a whipstitch is a lot like sewing with a running stitch.

1. Starting about 1 cm (½ in.) from the edges of the fabric, poke the threaded needle up through the fabric until the knot catches. Then, bring the needle around the fabric edge and poke it back through the other side of the fabric again a little way over.

2. Continue sewing in this way, keeping your stitches as even as you can.

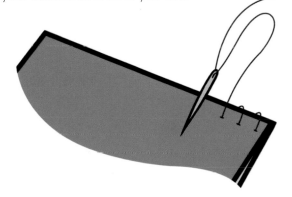

SEWING TIP:
If you've sewing by hand, slip a thimble onto the finger of your other (non-needle holding) hand to protect yourself from needle pricks.

# RSF, WSF, RSTOG, WSTOG TRANSLATION, PLEASE!

**RSF = Right side facing**
The right side, or good side
of the material, faces you.

**WSF = Wrong side facing**
The wrong side, or underside
of the material, faces you.

**RSTOG = Right sides together**
The right sides of two pieces of
material are placed together.

**WSTOG = Wrong sides together**
The wrong sides of two pieces of
material are placed together.

# UPDO IT

Ho-hum about your HAIR?
Need to SWANK it up for a special OCCASION?

*Whether your 'do is short 'n' sassy or long 'n' luxurious,
you're gonna want to check out this section for*

 a WOVEN *wonder of a* HAIR BAND
*to control even the unruliest 'do*

 HAIR STICKS *that'll really
stick it to a boring bun*

 a FAB *way to spiff up those
dull drugstore* HAIR COMBS

 *a reversible* PONYTAIL
WRAP *that doubles as a*
HAIR BAND — *and triples
as a little* SCARF

# Mane tamer hair band

*Tame your tangles and finesse your tresses
with a wickedly easy woven band.*

1 Measure and cut four 120 cm (48 in.) pieces of
different-colored ribbon.

2 On the cardboard or foam board, measure and mark
two lines that are 40 cm (16 in.) apart. Find the
center point between the lines
and mark another line.

16

HAIR gone HAYWIRE?    MOP gone MAD?

Get it UNDER CONTROL with this woven band ...

and LOOK LOVELY

while you're at it!

3 Using the center line as a guide, line the four ribbons WSF and centered on the cardboard. Make sure there are no gaps between them. Push a pin through each ribbon end to hold it in place on the cardboard.

4 Measure the width of the four ribbons together, then double this measurement. Cut a few pieces of the other four ribbons to this measurement.

5 Starting at the left line, weave a ribbon piece from step 4 WSF under and over the long ribbons. Add another ribbon piece under it, weaving over and under. Continue weaving ribbon pieces, cutting more as you need them, until you reach the line at the right end of the cardboard. Make sure there are no gaps between the ribbons.

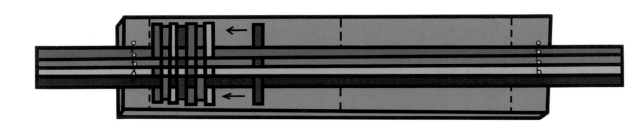

6 Cut a piece of iron-on adhesive that is 40 cm (16 in.) long and the same width you calculated in step 4.

7 Lay the iron-on adhesive paper-side up onto the woven ribbons. Follow the package directions to iron it on. Let cool and remove the paper backing.

**8** Fold the short ribbon edges over to meet in the center. Push a few pins into the board to hold the edges in place. Iron the edges down, removing the pins as you go. Let cool.

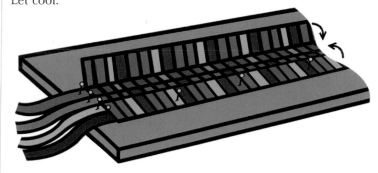

**9** Tie a small knot in each ribbon end to stop it from fraying.

To wear the hair band, gather the ribbons and tie them in a bow at nape of your neck.

## Kick It Up

Have short hair? Weave one for your waist, instead. Create a wild woven belt by measuring around your waist or hips and adding 80 cm (32 in.) for the length of the long ribbons.

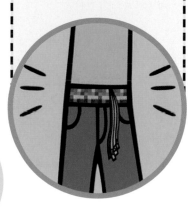

# Swish hair sticks

*Beautify a bun when you add wow to simple wooden chopsticks. Make 'em match or mix it up with different beads on each stick.*

1 Measure and mark about 20 cm (8 in.) from the point of each chopstick. Using a utility knife, carefully cut off the chopstick ends at each mark.

2 Apply an even layer of paint to each chopstick. Let dry. Repeat.

STUFF YOU NEED

• a pair of wooden chopsticks
• acrylic paint
• a glue gun and glue sticks
• two 7 mm (³⁄₈ in.) metal end caps
• two 5 cm (2 in.) eye pins
• a few beads
• two jump rings
• two charms
• a ruler or tape measure, a pencil, a paintbrush, a utility knife, needlenose pliers

STICK it to 'em with these STYLISH hair sticks.

21

**3** Apply a small dot of glue to the end of one chopstick and push a metal end cap onto it. Repeat with the other chopstick.

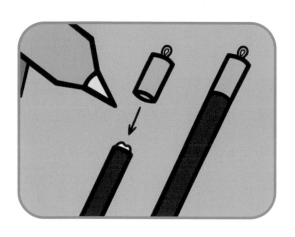

**5** Using the pliers, bend the straight end of the eye pin into an open jump ring. Use the pliers to close the eye pin loop. Slip the jump ring onto an end cap ring. Use the pliers to close the loop.

**4** Thread a few beads onto an eye pin, leaving 1 cm (½ in.) at the top.

**6** Open the bottom loop of the beaded pin a little bit. Slip a charm onto the loop. Use the pliers to close the loop.

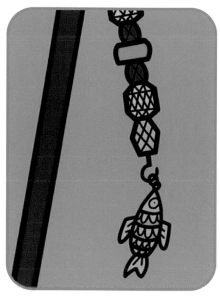

**7** Repeat steps 4, 5 and 6 to make a beaded pin for the other chopstick.

# Fab flower hair combs

*Take a trip from Dullsville to Style City when you add gorgeous hand-sewn flowers to inexpensive combs.*

**STUFF YOU NEED**

- tracing paper
- a small piece of fabric
- polyester stuffing
- two beads or buttons
- two hair combs
- a needle, and thread to match the fabric
- a ruler, a pencil, scissors, pins

1 Draw a 5 cm (2 in.) circle onto tracing paper and cut it out.

2 Lay the circle on the fabric and pin. Trace around the edge and cut out a fabric circle. Repeat to make another fabric circle.

Outgrown your FAVE piece of clothing? Use a swatch of it to make these FLOWERS and give it a NEW lease on LIFE!

**3** Lay the fabric circles RSTOG and pin. Sew the circles together with a 0.5 cm (¼ in.) seam, leaving 2.5 cm (1 in.) open. Remove the pins as you go.

**4** Turn the circle right side out. Push a small piece of polyester stuffing inside. Tuck in the fabric edges around the opening and pin. Using small stitches, sew the opening closed.

**5** Poke a needle and thread in the center of the circle and pull through the other side. Draw the needle around and back through the center of the circle again the same way. Pull the thread snug to create a dent. Repeat four more times around the edge of the circle to make five evenly spaced petals.

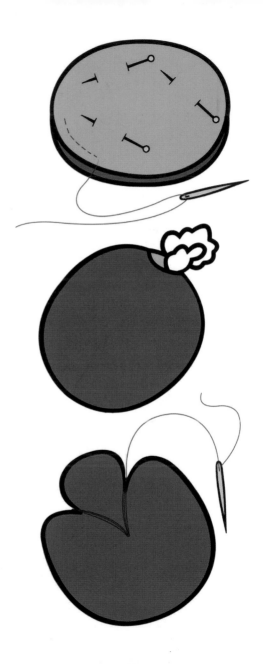

**6** Draw the needle through the center again and string a bead or button onto the needle. Poke the needle back down through the center. Sew a few more stitches through the bead or button. Tie a knot at the back of the flower.

**7** Position the flower on the top of one hair comb. Sew a few stitches around the middle of the comb's top edge and through the back of the flower. Tie a knot and trim the extra thread.

**8** Repeat steps 2 to 7 for the second comb.

## Kick It Up
Slip some of the flower fabric into the "Va-va-voom vinyl wristband" on page 32 and you'll have a perfectly pretty pair of accessories.

# Sassy ponytail wrap

*Tie it up or tie it down. This cutie-pie wrap can also be worn as a handy hair band or a sharp little scarf.*

STUFF YOU NEED

- 0.5 m (½ yd.) of fabric in two colors
- several beads
- a needle, and thread to match the fabric
- an iron and ironing board
- a tape measure, a pencil, scissors, pins

1 Measure, mark and cut a 7.5 cm x 77.5 cm (3 in. x 31 in.) piece of each fabric color.

2 Being careful to line up the edges, place the two pieces of fabric RSTOG and pin.

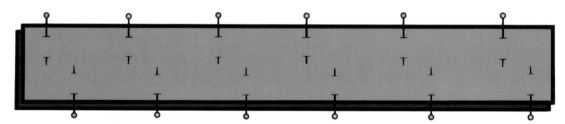

3 Measure 6.5 cm (2½ in.) from one top corner along the long edge and make a mark. Draw a line between the mark and the bottom corner on the same end.

4 Cut along this line. Repeat on the other end of the fabric, marking and cutting in the opposite direction.

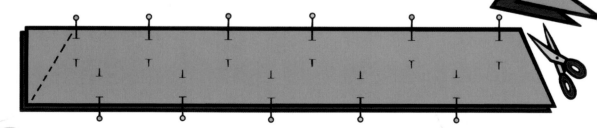

You'll get SIX FAB Looks in one with this wrap ...

THREE ways to wear it times TWO different CoLoRs!

29

5 Sew the pieces together with a 1 cm (½ in.) seam, leaving a 5 cm (2 in.) opening on one of the long sides. Remove the pins as you go.

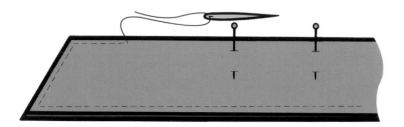

6 Turn the wrap right side out by pushing it through the opening. Use the pencil point to poke the corners out from the inside.

7 Tuck in the fabric edges at the opening and pin. Using small stitches, sew the opening closed, removing the pins as you go.

8 Iron the wrap flat.

9 Draw the needle and thread through one end point of the wrap. String a few beads onto the thread and then thread the needle back through all the beads except the last one you've added to make a beaded tassel. Sew a few stitches through the point of the wrap, tie a knot and trim off the extra thread. Repeat on the other end point of the wrap.

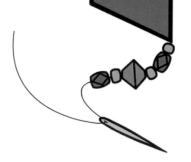

# FLASH IT

Feeling UNADORNED? Less than DAZZLING?
Wallet not up to a trip to the jewelry department?

Read on for some crafty — and cheap! — projects
to perk up your look:

 a vinyl **WRISTBAND** that's clearly
all about your unique style

 a **NECKLACE** that's definitely worth
the paper it's made of — and then some!

 a beautiful **BANGLE** that looks like
a million bucks but only costs a couple

 **RINGS** that'll make even diamonds
pale in comparison

 **EARRINGS** that really light up the night

# Va-va-voom vinyl wristband

*Simply slip in some punchy paper or some fab fabric — a piece to match your fave outfit, perhaps? — and you'll have a perfect personal style statement!*

1 For the length, measure around your wrist and add 5 cm (2 in.). Decide how wide you want your wristband to be. Measure, mark and cut your piece of paper or fabric to this length and width. If you are using fabric, cut it with pinking shears to prevent fraying.

2 Measure, mark and cut a piece of vinyl that is the same length as the paper or fabric piece and two-and-a-half times as wide.

3 Use a damp paper towel to wipe off any pen marks on the vinyl. Make sure it's dry before you continue.

These wrist wraps

are CLEARLY Cool.

33

4 Lay the paper or fabric WSF in the center of the vinyl, lining up the short edges.

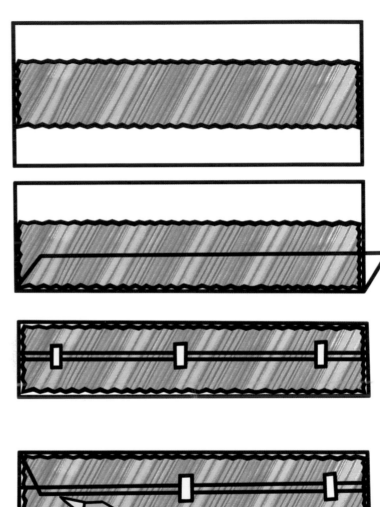

5 Fold over the long vinyl edges and overlap them so that the paper or fabric just fits inside.

Secure with a few pieces of masking tape.

6 Carefully glue the overlapped vinyl edges together, removing the tape as you go. Let dry.

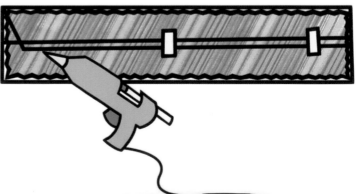

7 With the wristband WSF, measure and make a mark 1 cm (½ in.) in from the center of one short edge. Using a snap attaching tool and hammer, add the top half of a snap at this mark.

8 Turn the wristband over and repeat step 7 using the bottom half of the snap on the other short edge.

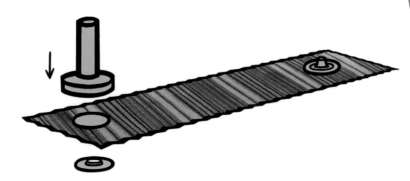

## Kick It Up

Ever pictured yourself as a superhero? Now's your chance to create a super identity! Make a sensation by drawing your own comic strip and turning it into a vinyl wristband.

35

# Pretty paper necklace

*These little beads are a snap to make. It's best to use paper that has a tiny pattern so it'll show when it's rolled up.*

1 On one of the blank piece of paper's short ends, measure and make a mark at 11 cm (4¼ in.). On the other short end, measure and make two marks: one at 9.5 cm (3¾ in.) and the other at 12 cm (4¾ in.). Join the three marks to make a triangle. Cut it out. This is your template for the large beads.

2 Lay a piece of patterned paper WSF. Lay the template on top along one edge and trace. Cut out the shape.

3 Starting at the wide end of the triangle, roll it tightly around the skewer. Dab a little Mod Podge under the end of the paper and press to hold the bead together. Paint the outside of the bead with Mod Podge. Remove from the skewer. Let dry.

STUFF YOU NEED

- a blank piece of paper at least 22 cm x 27 cm (8½ in. x 11 in.)
- three pieces of 22 cm x 27 cm (8½ in. x 11 in.) paper with different patterns
- a skewer or a round toothpick
- glossy acrylic sealer product, such as Mod Podge
- 18 beads
- beading wire, four crimps, a barrel clasp
- a ruler, a pencil, scissors, a paintbrush, a tape measure, needlenose pliers

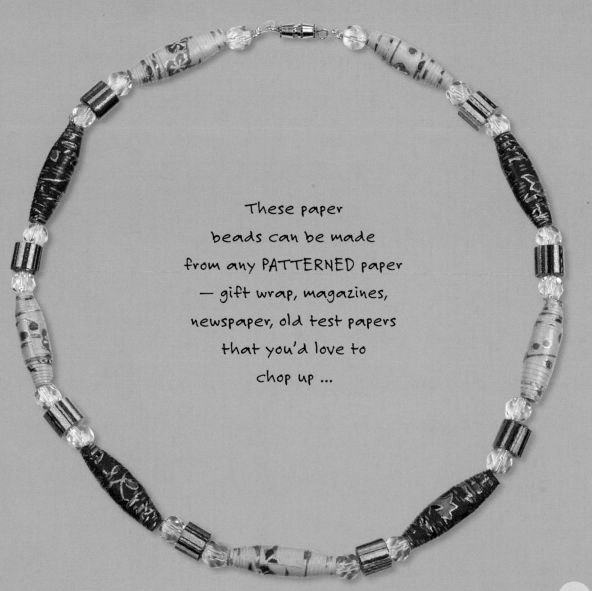

These paper
beads can be made
from any PATTERNED paper
— gift wrap, magazines,
newspaper, old test papers
that you'd love to
chop up ...

4 Repeat steps 2 and 3 to make eight more beads in different patterns.

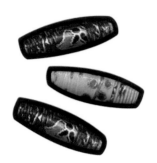

5 To make a smaller bead, measure, mark and cut out a piece of patterned paper that is 19 cm (7 ½ in.) long and 0.5 cm (¼ in.) wide. Roll it tightly around the skewer. Follow the instructions in step 3 to secure and paint the bead. Repeat to make seven more beads.

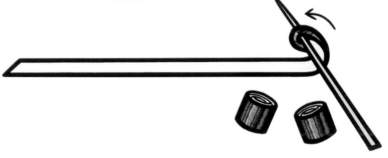

6 Measure around your neck and add 12.5 cm (5 in.). Cut a piece of beading wire to this length.

7 Thread two crimps and one half of the barrel clasp onto the wire. Thread the end of the wire back through the crimps to make a small loop. Using the pliers, squeeze the crimps closed. Trim off the shorter end of the wire as close to the crimps as you can.

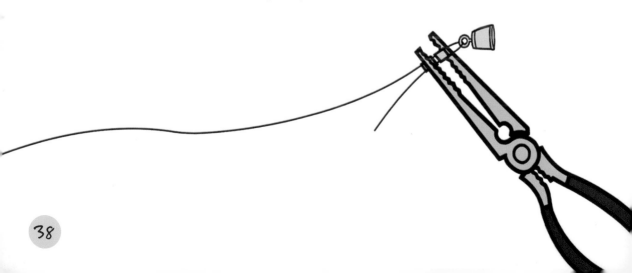

8  Thread the beads onto the wire in the pattern shown.

9  Repeat step 7 with the remaining wire end.

## Kick It Up

Make a couple of extra paper beads and whip up a pair of matching earrings! Thread the beads onto a 5 cm (2 in.) head pin, bend the straight end into a loop and attach it to an earring wire.

# Bonsai bangle

*This beauteous bangle was made with Japanese paper, but you can use any kind that suits your style — even magazine clippings or fancy gift wrap.*

STUFF YOU NEED

- a large cardboard mailing tube
- newspaper
- a few scraps of colorful paper
- white glue
- glossy acrylic sealer product, such as Mod Podge
- a ruler, a pencil, a utility knife, masking tape, a paintbrush, measuring cups and spoons, a small dish

1 Measure and draw a line 4.5 cm (1 3/4 in.) from one end of the mailing tube. Using the utility knife, carefully cut the tube along the line.

2 Slip the small piece of tube onto your wrist. If it is too large to stay on, use the utility knife to slice the tube open. Put the tube back onto your wrist and squeeze it until it's small enough to stay on but big enough to get on and off. Mark and trim the extra tubing.

3 Press the open ends of the tube together and stick a piece of masking tape around the front and back of the seam.

40

Astound your friends when you tell them that this fantastic bangle

was made of only cardboard and paper —
PRESTO CHANGE-O!

**4** Mix 250 mL (1 c.) of water with 25 mL (2 tbsp.) of white glue in a small dish.

**5** Tear some newspaper into 2.5 cm (1 in.) wide strips.

**6** Dip a strip into the glue mixture and wrap it around the tube, smoothing it as you go. Continue until you have about three layers of newspaper strips and none of the tube is showing. Let dry for 24 hours.

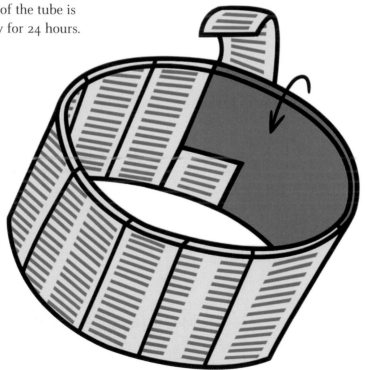

7 Cut or tear colored paper into 10 to 12 strips that are about 2.5 cm (1 in.) wide and 12 cm (4 3/4 in.) long.

8 Repeat step 4. Dip a colored strip into the glue mixture. Place it on the tube RSF, wrap the ends around the inside and overlap them. Continue adding strips, smoothing them as you go and overlapping them slightly, until the tube is covered. Let dry for 24 hours.

9 Paint a thick layer of glossy Mod Podge to cover the inside, outside and edges of the bangle. Let dry. Repeat twice.

## Kick It Up

Make a memory bangle of your friends. Cover it up with color-copied photos of your pals and paper strips of their autographs or sweet little notes to you.

# Rings that rock

*Pop in pics of anything that you love and rock the house with rings that show off the real you.*

STUFF YOU NEED

- one small sheet of thin Plexiglas, from the hardware store
- a small picture
- acrylic sealer product, such as Mod Podge
- a ring form
- a glue gun and glue sticks
- glitter, regular or ultra fine
- a cutting mat or other cutting surface
- a ruler, a pen, a utility knife, scissors, a small paintbrush, two small dishes

**1** Measure and draw a line 2 cm (¾ in.) from one edge of the Plexiglas.

**2** On the cutting mat and using a ruler as a guide, score the Plexiglas along the line with the utility knife 5 to 10 times.

**3** Place the Plexiglas on a table or countertop with the scored line along the edge. Gently press down to snap off a strip of Plexiglas.

who needs real jewels when you've got these ROCKIN' RINGS?

45

4 Repeat steps 1 to 3 to cut two 2 cm (¾ in.) squares from the Plexiglas strip. Remove any protective plastic covering from the Plexiglas.

6 Paint a layer of Mod Podge onto one Plexiglas square. Place the picture face up on top.

5 Place a Plexiglas square over the image you want to use, trace it and cut it out.

7 Paint a layer of Mod Podge on top of the picture. Then place the other Plexiglas square on. Using your fingers, press the layers together for a minute or two. Set aside and let dry.

8 Using the glue gun, apply a generous dollop of glue to the top of the ring form. Center the Plexiglas squares on the ring form, with the picture facing up. Let dry.

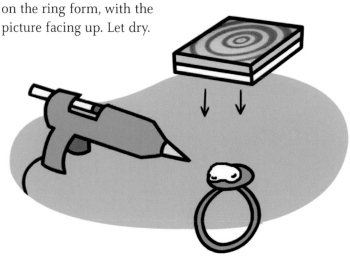

9 Put a little Mod Podge in a dish. Put a little glitter in another dish. Carefully dip the ring face's edges into the glue. Then, dip them into the glitter. Let dry.

## Kick It Up

Make Plexiglas charms with pics of your friends. Glue them onto small pendant forms instead of ring forms. Attach the charms to a chain bracelet and you've got yourself a charm-ing friends bracelet!

# Chandel-earrings

*You'll light up a room with these brilliant chandelier-inspired earrings!*

**STUFF YOU NEED**

- a package of jump rings
- needlenose pliers, wire cutters
- two hoop drops
- two lever-back earring wires
- six to eight head pins
- two large beads
- four to six eye pins
- several small beads
- about 10 cm (4 in.) of chain

**1** With the needlenose pliers, open a jump ring by gently pushing one end forward and one end back. Slip the ring onto the top loop of a hoop drop. Add an earring wire to the ring and pinch the ring closed with the pliers.

**2** To make the drop in the middle of the hoop, thread a head pin through a large bead and then through a small bead. With the pliers, bend the end of the head pin into an open loop.

**3** With wire cutters, cut a two-link piece of chain. Slip the chain onto the head pin loop. Pinch the loop closed.

48

Trip the light FANTASTIC

with EARRINGS that

light up the night!

4 Use a jump ring to attach the drop chain to the bottom loop of the hoop ring.

5 Use the small beads, head pins, eye pins, chain and jump rings to make six drops.

6 Attach each drop to the hoop and pinch the loops closed.

7 Make a second earring.

# Kick It Up

Make a matching — and stunning! — bracelet. Measure around your wrist and cut a piece of chain 1 cm ($\frac{1}{2}$ in.) longer. Make and attach a beaded drop to every link of the chain. Attach a clasp to one end of the chain with a jump ring. Then attach a jump ring to the other end of the chain to clip the clasp to.

# WEAR IT

GOT that "something's missing" FEELING when you go out?
OUTFIT lacking some OOMPH?

*Add a little ooh-la-la to your ensemble with these
must-have accessories:*

 *a reversible ribbon* BELT
*that you'll* FLIP *for*

 *a tulip* HAT *that* FLATTERS
*every face*

 *faux fur* CUFFS *that'll
add a dash of* FLASH

 *a* SASH *to add* PANACHE
*to any outfit*

# Belt-it-out belt

STUFF YOU NEED

*This belt's a little bit country and a little bit rock 'n roll. Wear it floral-side out when you want to be pretty and poetic, and then flip it to the sparkly side when you want to party it up.*

- a belt buckle with a 2.5 cm (1 in.) center post
- plastic jewels
- tweezers or needlenose pliers
- a glue gun and glue sticks
- two 1.5 m (1½ yd.) pieces of 2.5 cm (1 in.) wide ribbon in different colors or styles
- a needle, and thread to match the ribbons
- a tape measure, a pencil, pins, scissors

1 To glue the plastic jewels onto the belt buckle, hold each jewel with tweezers or needlenose pliers, apply a small dot of glue to it and gently press it onto the face of the belt buckle. Continue gluing jewels until the buckle is covered.

2 Measure around your waist or hips and add 25 cm (10 in.). Cut a piece of each ribbon to this length.

3 Lay the ribbons down WSTOG. Fold in the short edges of one end of each of the ribbons 1 cm (½ in.) and pin.

This DOUBLE-DUTY beauty can take you

from picnic to party with a SIMPLE FLIP.

53

**4** Sew the pinned edges together with a whipstitch (see page 13). Remove the pins.

**6** Pin the ribbons together along the length of the belt, folding in the short edges of the other ends 1 cm (½ in.).

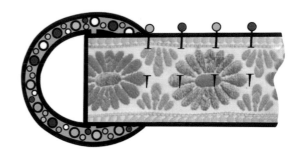

**7** Starting on one side about 0.5 cm (¼ in.) from the center post of the buckle, sew the ribbons together using a whipstitch along the edges. When you run out of thread, tie a knot between the ribbons and start sewing with a new piece of thread, positioning its end knot between the ribbons, too.

**5** Slip the sewn edge over the center post of the belt buckle so the ribbons are even on each side.

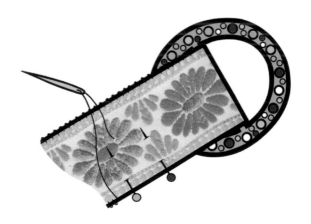

8 Continue sewing around one edge of the belt, along the short edge and back up the other side, ending about 0.5 cm (¼ in.) from the buckle's center post.

9 To wear the belt, flip the buckle to the side you want to face out and weave the belt end up through the buckle and back down through the other side.

# Too cute tulip hat

*Show your flower power when you sew up this cutie-pie hat in a charming tulip shape (a.k.a. a cloche).*

✳ *Note: You'll find the hat panel template on the inside back cover.*

- tracing paper
- 0.5 m (½ yd.) of tweed fabric
- a needle, and thread to match the tweed fabric
- small pieces of blue, yellow and orange felt fabric
- a pencil, scissors, pins

1 Photocopy the hat panel template, enlarging it by 200%.

2 Trace the template onto the tracing paper and cut it out.

3 Pin the template to the tweed fabric. Cut out the fabric around the edges of the template. Remove the pins. Repeat five more times so that you have six pieces in total.

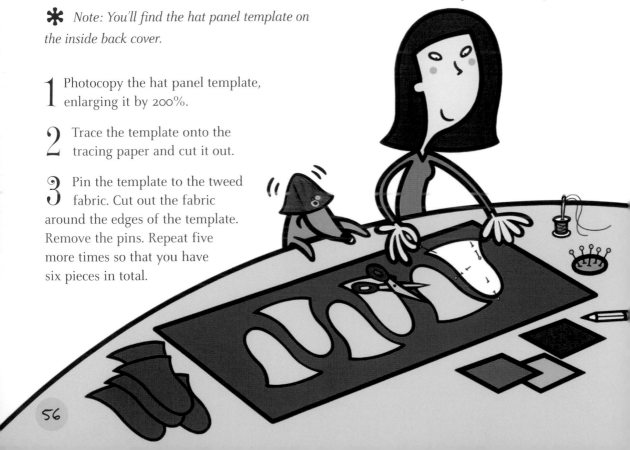

Tiptoe through the TULIPS ... HEAD and SHOULDERS above the rest!

4 Place two pieces of the tweed fabric RSTOG and pin along one long edge. Sew a 1 cm (½ in.) seam and remove the pins.

5 Pin another fabric piece RSTOG to one of the long open edges of the sewn piece from step 4. Sew a 1 cm (½ in.) seam, removing the pins as you go. This is half of the hat.

6 To make the other half of the hat, repeat steps 4 and 5 with the other three fabric pieces.

7 Place the two halves RSTOG and pin, leaving the bottom open. Sew a 1 cm (½ in.) seam, removing the pins as you go.

8 Fold the bottom edge of the hat over 2.5 cm (1 in.) and pin. Sew a 0.5 cm (¼ in.) hem along the cut edge of the bottom of the hat, removing the pins as you go. Turn the hat right side out.

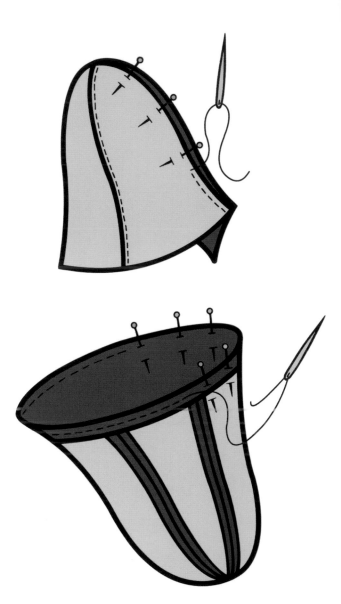

9 Cut a few different-sized circles from the blue, yellow and orange felt fabric to make a design that you like.

10 To attach the circles to the hat, sew an X through the center of each of the layers of circles, starting and ending on the inside of the hat.

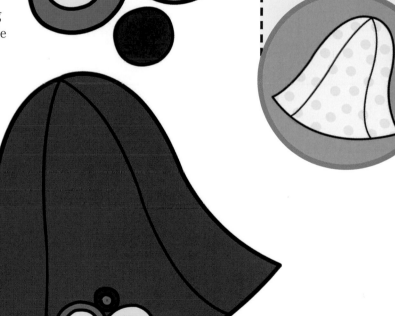

## Kick It Up

Beat the heat by stitching up a sweet summer tulip hat in a light cotton fabric.

# Superstar sweater cuffs

These kicky cuffs will make any sweater, shirt or jacket fun fur fabulous. Or simply snap one onto your wrist for a funky cuff bracelet.

STUFF YOU NEED

• 0.25 m (¼ yd.) of fun fur
• 0.25 m (¼ yd.) of felt
• a needle, and thread to match the fun fur
• two buttons
• two snaps
• a tape measure, a pencil, scissors, pins

1 Measure around your wrist and add 5 cm (2 in.).

2 Measure, mark and cut a piece of fun fur that long and 10 cm (4 in.) wide. Measure, mark and cut a piece of felt the same size.

Go from groupie to GLAM

with these STAR-INSPIRED cuffs.

**3** Pin the felt to the fun fur's furry side. Sew a 0.5 cm (¼ in.) seam around three edges, leaving one short edge open and removing the pins as you go.

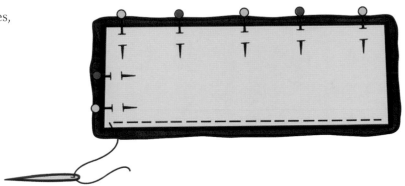

**4** Turn the cuff right side out. Tuck the open edges inside about 0.5 cm (¼ in.) and pin. Sew the opening closed using small stitches. Remove the pins.

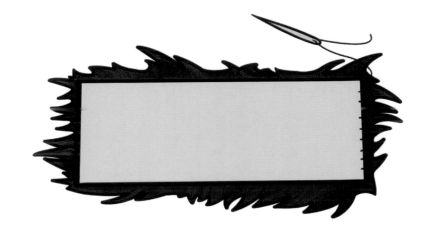

**5** Sew a button about 1 cm (½ in.) from the center edge of one short side of the fun fur.

**6** On the felt side of the cuff, measure and make a mark 1 cm (½ in.) in from the center edge of each short side.

**7** Separate the snap and sew one half at each mark.

**8** Repeat steps 1 to 7 to make another cuff.

# Oh-so-stylish obi

*If an obi looks good with a kimono, imagine the wow
it'll add to your T-shirt, skirt or dress!*

**STUFF YOU NEED**

• a 15 cm x 65 cm (6 in. x 26 in.)
  piece of fabric

• 2 m (2 yd.) of 1 cm (½ in.) wide
  ribbon

• a needle, and thread to match
  the fabric

• a tape measure, a pencil,
  scissors, pins

1 With WSF, fold one
long edge of the
fabric over 0.5 cm (¼ in.)
twice and pin. Repeat
along the other long edge.

2 Fold one short edge
of the fabric over
1 cm (½ in.) twice and
pin. Repeat along the
other short edge.

3 Sew around the obi edge, about
0.5 cm (¼ in.) from the edges,
removing the pins as you go.

Go from dull to DYNAMITE

when you tie on this
smashing OBI SASH.

**4** Measure and mark the center of each short side's inside edge.

**5** Fold and cut the ribbon in half. Fold and then pin one ribbon end WSF at one mark from step 4, about 1 cm (½ in.) from the obi edge. Sew the ribbon in place with a few stitches and remove the pin. Repeat to sew the other ribbon to the other end of the obi.

**6** Tie the obi around your waist, hips or chest, and trim the ribbon ends if you want them shorter.

## Kick It Up

Instead of trimming the ribbon ends, cross the ribbons at the back and tie them at the front, on top of the obi. "Sew" fab!

# STRUT IT

What's the FINISHING TOUCH to a SMASHING OUTFIT, you ask?

*A fab bag, of course! Don't leave the house without one of these in hand:*

 a MINI BAG *that* MAXES OUT, *doing it all and then some!*

 a BANGLE BAG *that holds your stuff and* ADORNS *your wrist — what more could you ask for?*

 *a hot-off-the-press* MESSENGER BAG *that really delivers the* NEWS

# Wee wonder bag

*This little bag can do it all. Tuck it into your purse or backpack to hold an MP3 player, a cell phone, your sunglasses or any other little things that need organizing.*

### STUFF YOU NEED

• 0.25 m (¼ yd.) of quilted fabric
• a needle, and thread to match the fabric
• a 20 cm (8 in.) zipper
• a handful of sequins and beads
• a tassel
• a tape measure, a pencil, scissors, pins

1 Measure, mark and cut a 20 cm x 25 cm (8 in. x 10 in.) piece of fabric.

2 Fold over one short edge 1 cm (½ in.) twice and pin. Sew a hem 0.5 cm (¼ in.) from the folded edge, removing the pins as you go. Repeat to hem the other short edge.

3 Fold the fabric in half RSTOG to match up the hemmed edges. Pin the sides.

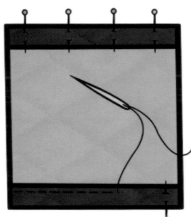

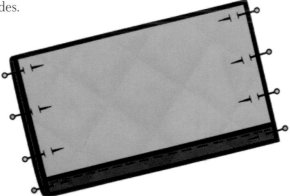

This HARDWORKING bag can PARTY, too —

as a POSH little PURSE!

4 Sew a 1 cm (½ in.) seam along each side edge, removing the pins as you go. Turn the bag right side out.

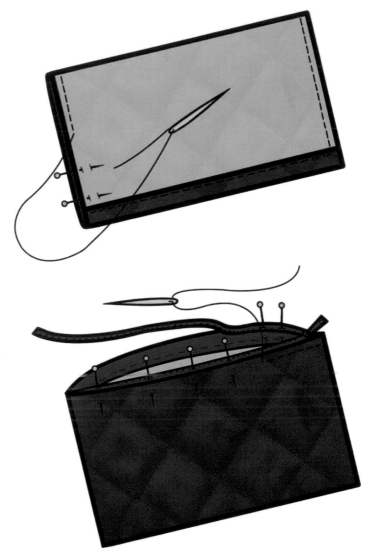

5 Open the zipper. Pin one zipper edge to the inside top edge of the bag. Sew the zipper edge in place following the line of stitches from step 2, removing the pins as you go. Repeat to sew the other zipper edge to the other top edge of the bag.

6 Poke the needle up from the inside of the bag at a spot where the quilted lines on the fabric cross. Add sequins and then a bead to the needle. Poke the needle back through the sequin and through the bag at the same spot you came up. Tie a knot and trim the thread. Repeat to sew sequins and a bead at each **X** where the quilted lines cross.

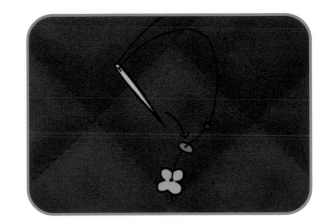

7 Slip a couple beads and sequins onto the tassel loop. Thread the loop through the hole in the zipper pull. Then, tuck the tassel through the loop and pull it tight.

# Bangle wristlet

*Slip this sassy sac onto your wrist and you've got the perfect combination of jewelry and a handbag.*

1 Measure, draw and cut a 22 cm x 24 cm (8 ½ in. x 9 ½ in.) piece of paper. Fold the paper in half and then in half again. With scissors, round off the corner that is not folded. Unfold the paper. This is your pattern.

2 Fold the fabric in half. Lay the pattern on top and use a few pins to keep it in place. Cut out the fabric pieces. Remove the pins and pattern.

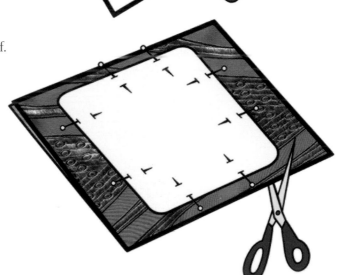

Here's a SLEEK little BAG that holds all the necessities for a night out —

and DECORATES your WRIST, too!

**3** Cut a 1 m (1 yd.) piece of bias tape. Starting at one side of a fabric piece, slip the fabric edge between the two layers of the bias tape and pin. Continue pinning bias tape around the fabric edges. Fold the end of the bias tape under and pin it to overlap the start of the bias tape, then sew, removing the pins as you go.

**4** Repeat step 3 with the other fabric piece.

**5** With WSF, pull a shorter edge of one fabric piece through a bangle. Fold the fabric edge down 5 cm (2 in.) and pin it evenly across the width of the fabric. Tuck in the bias tape edges on the inside of the bangle.

**6** Sew the fabric edge with a 1 cm (½ in.) hem, removing the pins as you go.

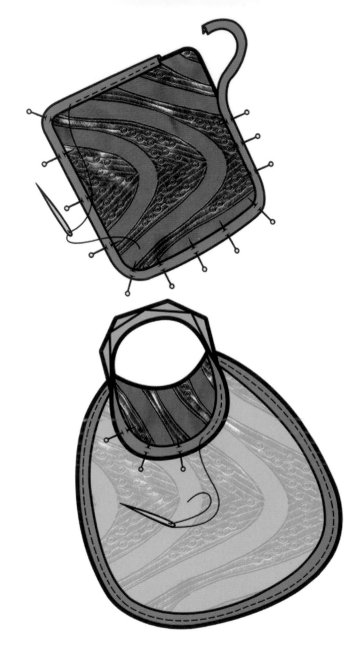

**7** Repeat steps 5 and 6 with the other fabric piece and bangle.

**8** Lay the fabric pieces RSTOG and pin them along the edges.

**9** Starting about 10 cm (4 in.) from the top of the bag, sew down the side, across the bottom, and up the other side of the bag, ending about 10 cm (4 in.) from the top of the bag. Remove the pins. Turn the bag right side out.

## Kick It Up

Make a spiffy shoulder bag by creating a bigger pattern and using bamboo rings for the handles.

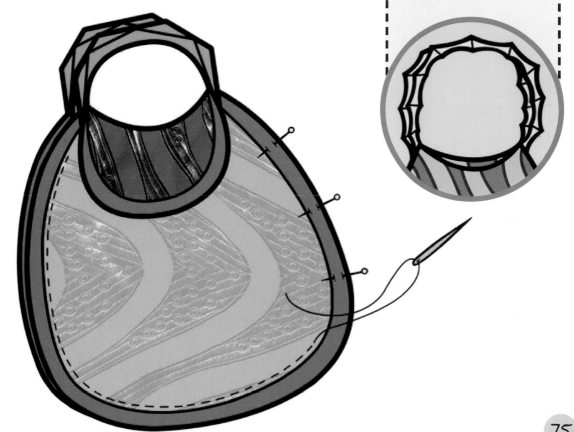

# Newsworthy bag

*Good news travels fast — and with this newspaper-and-duct-tape messenger bag, it also travels in style!*

**STUFF YOU NEED**

- newspaper
- clear duct tape
- a small square of peel-and-stick Velcro
- a tape measure, a pencil, scissors

1 Measure, mark and cut a 27 cm x 33 cm (11 in. x 13 in.) piece of newspaper.

2 Measure and cut a piece of duct tape that is about 30 cm (12 in.) long. Stick the tape along one short edge of the newspaper. Cut another piece of tape the same length and stick it below the first piece so that the tape edges are touching. Continue adding tape pieces to cover the entire side of the newspaper.

3 Turn the newspaper over. Repeat step 2 to cover this side with tape. Trim around the edges of the newspaper to cut off the extra tape.

4 Repeats steps 1 to 3 to make another tape-covered piece of newspaper.

RESCUE some NEWSPAPER from the recycling bin

and REUSE with STYLE!

5 For the strap, measure, mark and cut four 5 cm x 50 cm (2 in. x 20 in.) pieces of newspaper.

6 Starting with one strap piece, measure, cut and stick pieces of tape that are about 7.5 cm (3 in.) long across the width of the newspaper. Add the other pieces of newspaper to the end of the strap as you go to make a 2 m (80 in.) piece of strap. Turn the strap over and cover the other side with tape.

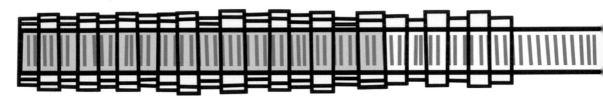

7 Trim around the edges of the newspaper to cut off the extra tape.

8 Stick one piece of duct tape along the length of the strap. Turn the strap over and repeat.

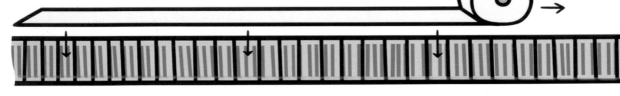

9 Measure and cut a 27 cm (11 in.) piece of tape. Overlap half of the tape's width onto one short edge of one of the newspaper pieces from steps 1 to 4. Flip the newspaper piece over, then stick the strap along the other half of the tape, lining up the strap and bag edges and centering the strap seam.

10 Fold the strap along the taped edge to make a crease.

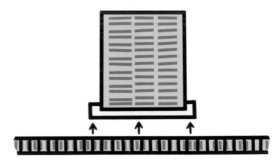

**11** Line up the edge of the strap with one long edge of the newspaper piece. Measure and cut a 33 cm (13 in.) piece of tape. Overlap half of the tape's width onto the strap.

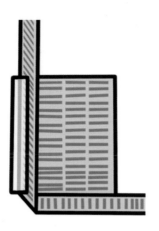

Flip the whole thing over and press the other half of the tape to the newspaper piece.

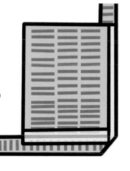

Repeat for the other half of the strap, and then flip the whole thing over again.

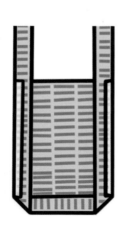

**12** Line up one of the long edges of the other newspaper piece to the strap. Measure and cut a 33 cm (13 in.) piece of tape and tape the strap and newspaper piece together.

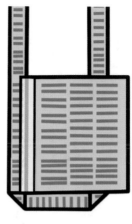

Repeat for the newspaper piece's other long edge.

**13** Measure and cut a 27 cm (11 in.) piece of tape to tape the bottom edge of the newspaper piece to the strap to create a box shape.

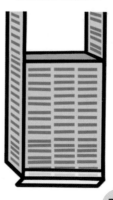

**14** Overlapping the strap ends by 5 cm (2 in.), tape them together.

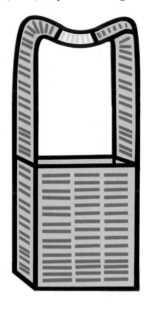

**15** For the closure, measure, mark and cut a 5 cm x 9 cm (2 in. x 3 ½ in.) piece of newspaper. Cover both sides with duct tape and trim off any extra tape around the edges.

**16** Fold the closure in half. Center the fold over the top of the bag opening. Use a few pieces of tape to stick one side of the closure to the bag.

**17** Separate the Velcro and stick one half to the inside of the closure, about 1 cm (½ in.) from the center of the open edge. Stick the other half of the Velcro to the bag to line up with the closure half.

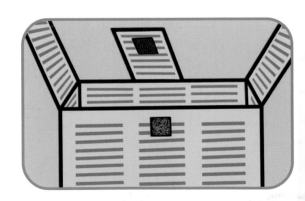